CW00920568

Social Science Research Methods in Contemporary Liturgical Research: An Introduction

by

Trevor Lloyd
Former member of the Church of England Liturgical Commission

James Steven
DMin Programme Director and Lecturer in Theology and Ministry,
King's College London.

Phillip Tovey
Director of IME (1-7) for Licensed Lay Ministers, Diocese of Oxford,
and Liturgy Tutor, Ripon College Cuddesdon.

Contents

ACKNOWLEDGMENTS
We want to thank the Alcuin/GROW Joint Editorial Board for
their encouragement in the production of this project as a
Joint Liturgical Study.

THE COVER PICTURE
shows a collection of research papers in this area.

First Impression May 2010

ISSN 0951-2667

ISBN 978-1-86825-047-5

1. Preface

Why don't people do more research on liturgy that focuses on people rather than on history, texts or language? With any research it is always important to be aware of what motivates the researcher – and it is helpful if the researcher states this openly. It might be a local vicar trying to gain support for a particular new policy on an aspect of worship, or a new incumbent genuinely wanting to discover the different experiences members of her congregation have, or an MA student who has chosen to do some research into people's feelings in worship and is now worried in case his selection of people, questions and methodology do not stand up to the test of academic rigour. It might be a lecturer in worship wanting to test out if a theory about how people react to the exchange of the Peace is correct; if it is going to be produced as a paper at a conference or as a possible contribution towards a further degree, it is important to get it right.

This monograph reviews a number of different approaches and tools that can be used, deliberately provoking questions such as 'Was the method chosen the most appropriate for the subject' 'Why was this method chosen rather than others? Was it because of cost, speed or simplicity in operation?' 'Would the conclusion have been different if a different research method had been used?' All of these are valid reasons for some situations, but it is as well to acknowledge them in an opening discussion on the choice of method. It is equally important to consider using more than one method. Why is it that different people sometimes get dissimilar results and interpretations from the same data or situation? Sometimes it is because they are using slightly different definitions, of categories of people for instance. Sometimes it is simply that time has moved on and events have changed the situation and those involved. But it may also be that two people are using different methods of research and so arriving at differing conclusions. One reason might be that the research is insufficiently objective; another might be a failure to look more widely at the subject using different tools. So look at what chapter two says on the importance of triangulation. No one method is sufficient, and by giving first-time researchers an overview or map of where they might go in choosing the tools they will use, this monograph may open some doors and indicate what to read next. But it will also give those who think they know what they're doing some markers against which to review their current practice!

One problem in research methods is language. We have already used tools, approaches and method. These and other terms are used in the literature but not always in a consistent way. We will try to use the terms in this way: philosophy is the theoretic approach you are taking to your research. It includes phenomenology, feminist, grounded theory and eclectic approaches. Methods are not restricted to one philosophy and includes issues such as quantitative, qualitative, ethics, triangulation. Tools, such as interview, questionnaire, survey and computer programmes can be used with any philosophy.

The monograph will also help those of us who are on the receiving end of such research, often in less academic fields, to evaluate its accuracy and substance. Sometimes you can't quite put your finger on why it is that you don't really believe the results and conclusions...and it can all go horribly wrong: sometimes it is obvious, other times less so. The tendentious minister, for instance trying to prove people want his style of worship. He asks a limited selection of the congregation who share his views, the people he naturally talks to who have a similar background. We might laugh at this, but he just might fail to realize how inappropriate it is to do a paper-based questionnaire on whether it is good to have substantial amounts of prayers, psalms and responses said corporately by the congregation in a situation where many find reading difficult. Or questions are phrased in such a way as to leave no room for the via media: 'Do you prefer the choruses we now sing or would you rather the choir sang in Latin?'

Example
The Area Dean sits on the Diocesan Board of patronage, responsible for appointments. He is anxious to show that in a benefice of six parishes all want a certain kind of churchmanship, and offers to 'do a bit of informal research' when he takes their services during the vacancy. He chooses carefully those he asks; and he prefaces his question with 'Of course, it is much easier to get someone of an evangelical (or catholic) persuasion nowadays', and he then goes on 'Would you not agree that the most important thing for this church in its worship is the quality of the preaching ministry (or is maintaining the eucharist at the heart of the community's life)?' He gets the score he wants, but the committee fails to examine his methodology or to realize that single-question surveys are not a good basis for making appointments in complex situations.

So it matters. It matters because people's experience of worship, or their lives, or their futures, or the growth and well-being of the church can be changed by good or bad research. But it matters most because research is about getting at the truth, telling it how it is, telling how people think, believe and behave in a way which they will recognize as the truth about themselves. It is the truth which will lead to changes in them, in their churches and in other churches, in teaching institutions and places where policy is made, which will bring glory to God.

2. Introduction: Social Science Research Methods and Liturgy

From its historical and pastoral roots liturgical studies has developed to include research of a more social scientific nature, partially to examine current phenomena and also to look at traditions that are 'free' with no set written texts. Thus a number of books have been published examining liturgical phenomena in the contemporary church. Some examples of this are: Albrecht (1999) who wrote a study of worship in Pentecostal and Charismatic churches, Stringer (1999) with an ethnographic study of churches in Manchester, McGrail (2007) on First Communion rites in the Roman Catholic Church, Tovey (2009b) examining the practice of extended communion, and Steven (2002) looking at charismatic worship in the Church of England. These all study worship from a social science perspective but use different approaches. The variety of different approaches can be quite daunting for the beginner in the field.

While there are many helpful books on social science methods, there are very few that apply this to theological studies in general and liturgical studies in particular. This monograph does not attempt an exhaustive study of different philosophies and methods of social science. Such work has already been written, for example Bryman (2004), and others mentioned below. Anyone planning a research project using social science methods will need to look at these textbooks and glean wisdom from them. This monograph aims to sit alongside such textbooks, giving particular information on how social science methods are related to liturgical studies. The connection is not always apparent at the beginning and can make the research seem more complex than it really is. This chapter will bring out some of the key issues that the researcher needs to be aware of from the beginning.

Practical theology and congregational studies are parallel fields in which social science methods are increasingly used, e.g. Cartledge (2003). One important book on methodology is Swinton & Mowat (2006), who look at the relationship of practical theology and qualitative research, drawing on projects with differing approaches. There are important methodological questions about the relationship of social science research to theology and scholars have different answers. In part this is a small section of the wider debate between the relationship of science and religion, and of the status of revelation compared to scientific method. Some approaches continue to give a priority to theology, others see theology and science as parts of the wider picture, as, e.g., Davies (2002). One short work looks at the issues between social sciences and liturgical studies (Mitchell, 1999), and one essay looks at a particular method (Johnson, 2005). While some theoreticians have exhorted liturgists to study the worship event (Hoffman, 1987), little has been written on the methodologies of this type of liturgical research. So the textbooks on social science methods exist but this monograph aims to make the connections with liturgical studies.

The new researcher

Beginning a project of study leads quickly into a large number of concepts and thoughts. The difficulty of this field of social science is that it is full of competing philosophies and a vast number of methods and tools. Words like quantitative and qualitative research, triangulation, ethnography, grounded theory, phenomenology, leap out of the page as the researcher begins to read the textbooks. At this point a brief introduction to some of the key issues is important.

The first thing about any research is to be very clear about what you are trying to study. This might sound obvious but it is a vital question. It is easy for a project to grow out of hand as more interesting questions come to mind. As you discover more information, other impinging issues will become clear and they provide further avenues of study. Most people overestimate what they need to do and quickly have projects that would be more than enough for three PhD's. Keeping your eye focussed on the issue and refining the research questions into a narrower and clearer aim is a key part of any research. While there is little more to say about this, it will in fact be one of the main issues in any project. This is why it is important to have someone else to talk to about the project, either a supervisor or a colleague in the ministry team for example. A person who can be a critical friend is worth their weight in gold.

One fundamental distinction is between quantitative and qualitative research, although there are crossovers between the two. Some research looks to study large populations and conduct statistical analysis of the responses. This can be in a number of areas. A few churches employ statisticians to collate and analyse data concerning the church. One example of this is the statistical unit of the Church of England, which provides information on church attendance, numbers of baptisms confirmations and a range of statistical data (Research and Statistics Department of the Archbishops' Council, 2004). Similar work is done on other churches as in the work on the Roman Catholic Church in England and Wales (n.d.). It may be that your project will use some of the information gathered in this way.

Other people make use of long questionnaires, which are then analysed to gather statistically valid information. One branch of practical theology, which sometimes calls itself empirical theology, particularly has emphasized this approach. Such quantitative research has been used to study a number of areas, for example in relation to grief and funerals (Quartier et al., 2004), to women in ministry (Robbins, 2001), and to personality and glossolalia (Francis & Robbins, 2003). The use of such an approach usually requires advanced knowledge of statistical computing software and statistical theory. It may be that you have these skills or it may be that you will have to go on specialized courses to gain them; many universities run courses to equip people in these areas. The difficulty with this research is you need a large sample and it can be time-consuming.

Other projects take qualitative approaches looking at particular examples and using the data to ask questions about the whole. One example of this is a study of one parish and its use of extended communion (Mills, 2006). Swinton & Mowat have looked at qualitative approaches in some detail. The researcher may be studying their own church and be engaged in participant research. This will need careful thinking about to foster objectivity and to be aware of the impact of the research on the community. Sometimes asking questions unmasks an issue under the surface. It may be that some people would prefer them to remain hidden. However a detailed investigation of one area can be of significance to the whole and this should not be underestimated when beginning research.

A key concept and part of your research design is triangulation. This is an important concept in quantitative research. Looking at an issue from a number of directions can confirm and question assumptions and conclusions. For example, while a parish may ask the bishop for a lay person to be licensed to conduct extended communion for the purposes of the residential homes, the service data over many years from the register may suggest that another important feature has been to cover clergy holidays. Gathering data from more than one source is an important part of a project. It provides the depth of data sometimes called a 'thick description' in order to come to understanding of the phenomena you are studying.

Philosophical approaches and methods

The new researcher is confronted with a variety of philosophical and ideological approaches. Different researchers use different methods to conduct their research. It is worthwhile looking at some of these differences and trying to understand their significance. It is not possible to explain all these approaches here and this is an exercise that happens more fully in the textbooks. What is perhaps more helpful is to point to some liturgical studies research that has employed different approaches.

The list of philosophical approaches is large but some of the more important approaches are:

- Phenomenology; e.g. Savage (2001) on collects and Wolff (1999) on televised worship.
- Anthropology; e.g. Stringer (1999) on churches in Manchester.
- Sociology; e.g. Flannagan (1991) on various aspects of ritual, and Turner & Edgley (1976) on funerals
- Grounded Theory; e.g. Cheetham (2001) on worship in schools.
- Feminist; e.g. Ramshaw (1996) on language and Garrigan (2004) who includes some studies of women's communities
- Queer; e.g. Stuart (2000) looking at Diana's funeral
- Inculturation; e.g. Tovey (2003) on the eucharist in Africa and Pitts (1993) on Afro-Baptist Worship.
- Narrative; e.g. Yust (2006) looking at congregational consultation.

It is important to understand the background to these various approaches and it might be that you may want to follow one strictly, but in reality many people take a more eclectic approach and combine important points from various philosophies.

Alongside the philosophies are a number of tools. These include the use of questionnaires, interviews, documentary analysis, analysis of on-line material, and observation. Some of these will form chapters in the rest of this monograph. You will need to think through which tools are most appropriate for your study and you may have to pilot some of them first to see what is the best way to collect the data you want. Some objects of research require one particular tool but in many research projects you could involve more than one approach. You need to think about what philosophy is most appropriate for your research. It is also important to think of the ethical implications of your approach and of whom you are working with e.g. there are specific issues in conducting interviews with children. This will also be discussed briefly in a later chapter.

3. Literature Review and Document Analysis

Questions for a research project may come from pastoral work or may come from reading books that spark ideas and questions. The literature review is often seen as a way of having this wider discussion.

In liturgical study the literature review can be quite broad. There is a whole variety of different types of material to consider, including:
- Textbooks often looking at a topic e.g. eucharist or baptism.
- Liturgical texts by the churches (denominational, national, or local)
- Hymns books
- Commentaries on the liturgy
- Denominational reports, which often show some of the principles incorporated in the liturgy
- Articles on results of liturgical research
- Service registers
- Records of Synod debates
- Synod papers, reports from revision committees
- Diaries

Some of these may be easily available others may take some searching out. Increasingly Church of England General Synod material is online, which brings up another source of information, online and web-based data. This is very diverse in nature but can include service rotas, circuit plans, local church records of meetings, parish websites, diocesan policies. There are increasingly books available on line.

There are textbooks that look at the literature review and direct you as to how to analyse the data you gather, one such book is Hart (1998). It is essential to read up similar pieces of research to what you intend to do. It can either be on a similar topic or it might be using the methodology you have chosen but in a different area. Both in terms of either method and or subject there is likely to be some else who has conducted some research. It is also important to evaluate the research of others and consider how this will influence what you do, and include such evaluation in your own research.

Example of Young on daily prayer
Young centred his research on the practice of the Daily Office in the

Diocese of London, which is available in a dissertation (Young, 2008a) and in summary form in an article (Young, 2008b). This he did by a web-based search, questionnaire and interviews. His literature review is at the beginning of the dissertation. Here he carefully goes through the liturgical changes to the Daily Office in the Church of England and reviews the main textbooks and writings on the office. He notes that history has been the main paradigm of many of the experts and that little work has been on the actual practice of the office. It is this observation that drives the rest of his work. 'What actually happens?' and 'what is appropriate use of the office as mission?' are two key questions for him. He uses the interviews to give examples of a positive use of the daily office for laity and for mission, and suggests ways forward. Here is an example of the integration of the literature review in a piece of work. Indeed here it drives the research in an empirical direction by noting a gap in the literature.

Books that discuss research will also look at documentation e.g. Bryman (2004). Some books that go on to discuss writing the report will include helpful suggestions on literature review (Wolcott, 1990) as do more generic books on research (Bell, 2005). One of the key questions at this point is of access to libraries and the internet. Nowadays you ideally need to be well connected to both for your research project to flourish.

Example from Guiver on daily prayer
One of the textbooks on daily prayer, *Company of Voices*, includes a chapter on the eighteenth century. In this chapter a wide range of documentary sources are used to build up a picture of church life. The sources include letters to *The Guardian* and *The Spectator*, a published letter, Pepys' diary, a biography of a cleric, and service registers. This is a wide range of evidence brought together to demonstrate the place of daily prayer in the churches of London.

In a more contemporary study a similar diversity of evidence could be drawn on to illustrate the worship life of a contemporary church. There are perhaps fewer letters to national newspapers, but church papers frequently have letters and articles on worship. Of particular interest is also *News of Liturgy*, which ran from 1975 to 2003 and is now searchable online, and *Praxis News of Worship*, which is also specifically on worship issues.

Documents in Liturgical Studies

There may be a rich set of documents for examining a local church in an area of liturgical study. This includes service registers, local texts, church and parish magazines, the circuit plan, web-based material, newsletters, notice boards, and church committee records.

One key document in the Church of England is the parish profile. A parish has to write a profile each time there is a vacancy, a legal requirement if the parish is not suspended (Harries, 1995). These profiles give a snapshot of the parish and are an element of corporate self-understanding. They include data about services, but they may not be very accurate about occasional services. They will usually however contain the idealized rota of services, before all the exceptions change the order.

Another significant set of documents is the service booklets that parishes have produced. In churches that use a written liturgy, the expectation of worshippers may be to be given a service book and hymnbook at the door. Some parishes have a variety of such services, not least for Family Services. There are a variety of interests from looking at local texts. Many are customized and edited service booklets based on denominational texts. Some have merely simplified the authorized text but many have edited further. For Services of the Word, the freedom available has given rise to considerable local expression. Some new texts may in the future become a part of the 'official' liturgy of the church. All of this can be indicative of local theology (Schreiter, 1985) and is possibly a neglected documentary source (cf. Cameron, 2005). However, there may be critical differences between the written text and its performance (Garrigan, 2004).

Example of Family Services

In 1984 Chelmsford ran a diocesan survey on Family Services, which was at that point a growing service (Ashton, 1984). They asked that people send in examples of what they were doing alongside the results of the questionnaire. They received 106 orders of service. They analysed the sources of the different services and collected examples of prayers in various parts of the service. Theological questions were raised about various texts that they discovered.

They also collected information on hymnbooks that were used, 26 in all, the majority using material from the *Ancient and Modern* tradition. Moreover analysis of the service sheets showed that the lectionary was rarely used in this type of service.

Many denominations keep service registers, which record the type of service, the number of people attending, and maybe some age information. Cameron (2005) comments:

> For many practical purposes recent church registers and records are invaluable for accessing the numbers attending and nature of services (p.28).

Each time a service is conducted in the Church of England it is recorded in the register with the number of people attending. This is a potentially rich mine of information but has various problems. First, this is a private document and permission has to be gained for its use (Legal Advisory Commission of the General Synod, 1997). Then the recording of the type of service might not be very accurate. Also the recording of the numbers might not be exact and the accuracy may vary from church to church. Finally, if there are a number of signatures it might not be easy to discern who were the leaders of the service, a problem of legibility.

Further problems may arise in accuracy. Tovey (2009c) found in his study of extended communion that the names in the register were hard to read and that it never said extended communion. The result was that the register appeared to suggest that there was lay presidency happening in the churches he studied. It was only in talking over the register with someone from the local church that he was able to ascertain who the leaders were and which services were extended communion.

Congregational studies look at particular churches to understand how they work. One key area in this is the worship, as churches are worshipping communities. Some congregational studies suggest classifying a church in a totemic typology (Hopewell, 1987). Other approaches might stress local theology as ordinary theology (Astley, 2002) and assert its importance (Astley & Christie, 2007). Documentary evidence is one key aspect of this type of research.

Diversity of documentary evidence is important in any project. While the profile may give the idealized worship-rota, the pew-sheet will say what was planned for that day, and the service book records what happened. All sorts of factors may lead to changes in the programme, even at the last minute. What's more, aspirations and theories may be espoused in documents and in interviews, but the translation of this into practice may show other factors as important. Contrasting views in, say, the service record to the parish profile can indicate gaps between theory and practice that may lead to further questions and lines of investigation.

4. Surveys and Questionnaires

Many pieces of liturgical research involve a survey or questionnaire, e.g. on communion before confirmation (Kay et al., 1993), or on children's sermons (Sims, 1999), or on preaching (Ross, 1995). This can be an excellent way of finding out information from a number of people. You can ask the same series of questions to a group of people and come to conclusions about their thoughts, values and practices. You may well have been asked to participate in surveys for marketing purposes, perhaps with the sweetener of your name going into a prize draw. There is much good advice in the basic textbooks about this and it is worth spending the time reading up about questionnaires, e.g. in books on research methods (Bryman, 2004) or specifically on questionnaires (Oppenheim, 1966, 1992). There are many different types of question that you can ask and methods of asking them (Gillham, 2000). It is important to get your questionnaire right for your particular research. The last thing you want to do is to send something out and then discover that a vital question has been missed out, so it is worth testing it with three or four people first. Questionnaires are widely used and books on their use for teachers (Munn *et al.*, 1990), and nurses (Abbott *et al.*, 1998) may be of comparative help for liturgical researchers. People are often willing to complete questionnaires. The fact that they have completed a questionnaire is regarded as ethical consent to the process, but you do need to explain the purpose of the survey and what you will do with the information.

The questions
Most research is based on asking questions. You will need to think through exactly what you want to find out and what you are going to ask. There are a number of different types of questions. Some may be basic data, the age and gender of the respondents. Other questions may involve the respondent filling in a scale of, say, 1 to 5 on how they agree or disagree with a statement: this is called a Likert scale. There may be open questions where the respondent can put in their own words their view on a particular topic. Often even a questionnaire of only one side of A4 can include all of these types of question.

Some research is around finding out what people think, as, e.g., Bryant (1983) on attitudes to liturgical change with the introduction of the ASB; similarly regular surveys are conducted on people's belief in God. Others might look at patterns of behaviour, as, for example, where Bensen & Roberts (2002) looked at attendance patterns. Some surveys go beyond finding out what is there and test the theories of the researcher, e.g. in researching children's worship (Sims, 1999). Many questionnaires will do a mixture of finding out and testing theories. Turning your questions into theories that are testable focuses the piece of research you are conducting.

An example: Chelmsford Family Services

The working party set up in the diocese of Chelmsford to investigate Family Services, mentioned above (Ashton, 1984), employed two phases of research: first a questionnaire to all with pastoral responsibility (507); and a second phase of visits to parishes and a second questionnaire. The aim was to find out what was happening in parishes and make recommendations for this type of service.

In this second phase two deaneries were selected and the rural parishes of one episcopal area. In one deanery all the parishes were surveyed, in another eight representative parishes were visited, in the episcopal area three deaneries were covered but towns (and vacancies) were omitted. Part of the issue here seems to have been getting a balanced selection of rural and urban. It is important that the criteria for selection are clear. The mixture of approaches was taken: survey by post, telephone survey, observational visit. This made for a rich body of data that was able to look at the issue from a number of perspectives.

The first questionnaire was of two sides of A4 with 12 questions in all. The return rate was 64%. These were mostly questions of frequency or had yes-no answers, e.g.
- Do you have a non-liturgical service less than once a fortnight? A yes-no answer.
- What is the average attendance at your non-liturgical service? A space for a figure.
- How many baptisms were in your parish in 1984? Spaces for six age categories

Thus lots of 'hard' data were gathered but little of the opinions of leaders or participants. The questionnaire is included in the report (pp.42-43) as is collation of the data. The questionnaire also asked for people voluntarily to include examples of services that they were using. So a second element of data was collected alongside the questionnaire.

The second questionnaire ran to eight pages. This was more of a schedule of questions for interviews that were conducted within sample churches. Thus a classic pattern of wider questionnaire with follow-up interviews was conducted.

The report was to have an impact beyond the diocese. 73% of the parishes surveyed were found to be conducting Family Services, most frequently monthly. This was a much higher figure than people thought. While it was realized that Family Services had become popular, no one knew the full extent of the movement. The diocesan report was more widely read, and it contributed to the development of official provision of the Service of the Word.

The number of questions is important. People respond less well to a long complicated questionnaire that will take one hour to fill in, compared to something that only takes 15 minutes. You need to estimate how long it will take and warn people in advance. Those of you who have been telephone surveyed, being told that it will take ten minutes and finding it takes half an hour, will know how annoying that can be. A few well-worded questions can result in significant information. Badly worded questions can confuse the person being surveyed and this will lead to confusing responses. It is always worth piloting the questionnaire on some volunteers, asking for feedback on the questions and thus learning whether the questions were clear. It is also worth considering how you handle those situations where people are not used to reading.

Hospice example

One children's hospice has been using a smiley face chart with the question 'Can you put a tick against the face which shows how you feel when you arrive at the hospice?' and faces ranging from very happy to very sad. This is followed by the question 'Can you put a tick against the face which shows how you feel when you leave the hospice?' This approach could clearly be developed for church services – and for adults, too!

Scope

The type of research is also an important question. We have already seen how quantitative and qualitative research differ; questionnaires can be used in both. Some surveys are a part of a research project that aims to gather statistically significant data. This will tend to have a large number of questionnaires sent out and analysed. Some work is done by statistical departments of denominations, who then produce reports of the state of the denomination, e.g. for the Roman Catholic Church (The Catholic Church in England and Wales, 2007), or the Church of England (Research and Statistics Department of the Archbishops' Council, 2004).[1]

Some university-based theologians have conducted surveys of numbers of people to find out particular aspects of interest, e.g. on baptismal policy (Francis et al., 1996), or on gender issues (Robbins, 2001). Those who use such methods may call their work empirical theology and see this as a particular type of practical theology. University-based theologians tend to sample people to survey in statistically sound ways to be able to draw empirical conclusions.

There are however qualitative ways of using samples and questionnaires. You may be asking for opinions of people in one church, or across a benefice or deanery. Here you may simply post the questionnaire to all on the electoral roll, or give the survey out on one Sunday, or email it to people, or invite them to join an online survey. Different methods will produce different responses. You need to think through quite carefully what is the best method.

Example: Bowsher on Christenings
A parish-based example can be seen in the surveys of Andii Bowsher on christenings and the language of baptism (Bowsher, 2004). This was work conducted by a parish priest rather than a university-based theologian. In this research he gave out a short questionnaire to those enquiring for the christening of their children. The questionnaire asked 'in asking for your child to be christened, how important to you is...?' – and nine options were then given:
- wanting to celebrate the birth of your child
- introducing your child to church
- giving thanks for a safe delivery
- giving thanks for the child himself or herself
- family tradition or pressure
- asking for God's blessings on him/her
- naming the child before God
- asking God's help to be good parents
- opening the door to Sunday school

---

[1] http://www.cofe.anglican.org/info/statistics/churchstats2007/statisticsfront.html . You can now access all the results from 2001 to 2008.

to be ticked on a scale of 1 to 4. This was given as a part of the baptismal interview. It was made clear that there were no right answers and that the baptism was not dependent on 'correct' responses.

The focus of the questionnaire was on their attitudes, the theory being tested is that the request for 'christening' does not necessarily mean a request for Christian baptism. The data were collected over eight years until about 100 responses were gained. It was conducted in four parishes by Andii Bowsher and four parishes by colleagues. The data are collected and analysed from a variety of perspectives.

While families come looking for something clear and decisive, the meanings discussed as most important were not baptismal in content. It would also appear that he did not find (grand-) parental pressure as a significant factor in the data. He suggests that this supports the rise in thanksgivings in the church.

This is an important piece of work from a minister. You do not have to be a professional researcher or part of a denominational project to take part in research that can produce significant results.

People are often worried about the response rate, thinking that it has to be high for the results to be valid. This may be true if you are looking to complete a statistically based piece of work, but some of the research that is discussed in the public arena is based on quite low response rates. It is quite important that you work out what percentage of your questionnaires has been returned. It might help you to sharpen your practice in the future. If you are sending a questionnaire out by post, then a stamped addressed envelope will get more returns. If you give a survey out in church, it is probably better to ask people to fill it in on the spot (but do give options for people not to participate).

Example: a local church questionnaire
INTERVIEW SHEET used by a North London church trying to find out what people thought of plans for all-age worship and teaching. Respondents were asked to circle their approximate age group and how long they had worshipped at the church, then to tick boxes for other questions, some of which were:

1 Would you be happier in a group where
   ☐ the leader does all the talking (as in the sermon at present)?
   ☐ there is time to discuss as well as listen?
   ☐ discussion takes most of the time?
2. Would you prefer people to be separated into age groups?
   ☐ Always
   ☐ Sometimes
   ☐ Never
3. Assuming you were able to join in the whole session, would it make much difference to your family routine if the Communion service started at 9 a.m., 9.15 a.m. or 9.30 a.m. ?
   ☐ No difference   Time preferred: ....
4. Do you agree with the suggestion that at 11.15 a.m. everyone (children included) meets together for a brief closing act of worship? This would prevent groups going on and on or becoming isolated from everyone else.
   ☐ Yes ☐ No ☐ Don't mind
5. What do you feel about these points in the suggested pattern?

	Good idea	Bad idea	Don't mind
+ six 5 week courses a year.	☐	☐	☐
+ everyone could have a programme card and choose which group to join each 5 week course, or simply come for a particular course which interested them.	☐	☐	☐
+ on the other Sundays the order of the Holy Communion service would be as at present.	☐	☐	☐

The nature of the questions is significant. If the questions ask about personal or controversial information, then people may only be willing to respond secretly. Indeed there are some subjects where people may be unwilling to complete a questionnaire and are happier to be interviewed. Sensitive issues are more difficult to research (Lee, 1993). An example of the effect of sensitive research on questionnaires can be seen in Tovey's research on extended communion (Tovey, 2009c). He conducted a pilot survey on extended communion but got very poor responses in his pilot, even when sending it to people who were well known to the researcher. Further reflection led to the conclusion that this was a sensitive topic in that there was a general feeling that it was 'not quite proper', particularly when it had not been authorized correctly or the extent of the bishop's permission was not clear. In this circumstance he found that interviews were better than a survey. Such factors can influence research and limit the efficacy of a questionnaire.

Example: the Methodist Church on Children and Communion
In 1997 the Methodist Church wanted to review its policy on children and communion (Methodist Church, 1997). It decided to send a postal questionnaire to a selection of ministers with questions of review. 390 ministers were selected and 324 replied, a very high response rate, perhaps indicating some ministerial interest in the question. They had also sent out a reminder letter where needed. Seven questions of policy and seven questions of local church practice were asked.
Is there a children in communion policy in place?
- What policy is in place?
- Who took the initiative for setting the policy?
- What reservations did churches have about the introduction of the policy?
- How was the policy received initially within the church?
- What impact did the introduction of the policy have on the congregation?
- What measures were thought to be important in the introduction of the policy?

Church Practice
- When are children present at some point during the service of Holy Communion?
- Which parts of the service are children present for?
- Where a family Communion is celebrated which service books are used?
- At what age do children share in different aspects of the service?
- Where conditions are specified before the elements are offered - what are they?
- What is the practice for administering the elements?

The questions were open in nature and so the responses were grouped into sets and percentages given of those that responded in similar ways. The responses were set out in a report to conference and published on the church website.

The survey was discussed in the context of research on their own policy and the policy of other denominations. As a result of the questionnaire, specific recommendations were made to change the policy of the Methodist Church. This type of research was concerned directly to influence the policy of a church. It may be that you wish to research something that may make a change in your congregation, or perhaps the church committee has asked for research on a particular question. This would be a scaled-down version of this Methodist approach.

Managing collation

In small-scale research it may be that you have 20-30 questionnaires that are returned. If your group is of a particular size, e.g. all the clergy of a deanery, or all the members of a church of 30 people, the numbers may be smaller. You will however have to collate the material once it is returned, and you might like to think about how you will do that before you send out the questionnaire. Questions that involve a response using a Likert scale (e.g. 1 to 5, agree to disagree) enable the conversion of the information into percentage of responses and then into charts, which can be a useful way of presenting the information. You will, however, have to spend time counting responses and collating open questions. Large-scale projects employ people to do such work; small-scale projects often have the researcher doing this work.

One of the advantages of an online survey is that the programme collates the information for you, without you having to type the results into a computer. This can save a lot of time, be economical as it needs no postage, and be conducted in quite a short period. The disadvantage is that it only works if your target group has high access to the internet; but a good example of this can be seen in an online questionnaire on the liturgical experience of Reader candidates prior to their selection (Tovey, 2009a). The online programme collated all the responses, which considerably speeded up the research project.

Follow up

It is quite common to follow up a survey with a set of interviews. This enables a second phase of the research. The interview will enable you to build on open questions, or ask further questions where the answers were unclear. What is important is that you ask people if they would be willing to be interviewed on the questionnaire. This may entail them ticking a box, if you know who they are, or, if the questionnaire is anonymous, them giving you some contact details on the questionnaire. This is another issue that you need to think through before you start the research.

5. Participant Observation

Traditionally the preserve of anthropologists studying tribal groups in distant lands, participant observation is now used to explore a wide variety of social settings in the modern developed world, ranging from education and businesses to ethnic groups and youth culture. Participant observation is often regarded as a hallmark of ethnographic research, ethnography being a form of social research used by a variety of scholars to study firsthand the experience and social interactions of human beings in order to develop an in-depth understanding of their culture.

Why Participant Observation?

The main advantage of participant observation, as Jorgensen argues, is that it provides 'a strategy for gaining access to otherwise inaccessible dimensions of human life and experience' (1989, 23). By participating in the ritual event of worship you are allowed access to two sources of knowledge. One is the practice of the worshipping community, knowledge of which is only reliably available when you have direct access to the event by means of participation. This is most obviously the case for worship that is embedded in an oral culture, such as within Pentecostalism, where there are no written texts or rubrics that constitute a reliable guide for the researcher. Less obvious, but no less significant, is the manner in which an authorized liturgical text is performed in a worshipping community, the details of which (including, for example, variations and additions to the text) are all only fully available by means of participation.

The second form of knowledge that is accessible through participation is what might best be called the tacit knowledge that is generated through participation in the ritual. The focus of attention here is not primarily knowledge about the events in worship but knowledge of what it is like to be a worshipper in this ritual environment. By taking stock of the existential experience of worship, you are given an invaluable means of understanding the dynamics of the rite and are one step closer to understanding the rite from an insider's perspective. Examples of the significance of this to studies on worship can be found in Stringer (1999) and in Steven (2002). In Stringer the exposure to an independent church's worship led him to experience the conversion narrative that was at the heart of the worship pattern of that church. The impact of the ritual sequence in a 'time of worship' on the researchers in Steven's study of charismatic spirituality was key to understanding the nature of the intimacy that was mediated by such ritual.

Participant observation is therefore a means of accumulating a deep knowledge of acquaintance; participation in a ritual will give us important insights into the nature of the rite and how it is experienced by the worshipping community. As the anthropologist Clifford Geertz admirably summarized, 'the trick is to figure out what the devil they think they are up to' (Johnson, 2005, p.212). This will, of course, take time, and the frequency and length of time to be spent on participant observation will be an important consideration when drawing up your initial research plan. However other more time-efficient methods, such as surveys and questionnaires, are no real substitute for the form of attentiveness that participant observation brings to the complexities, subtleties and richness of ritual and social interaction.

Relating to the Field of Study

In its simplest form the participant observer's relationship to the field of study can be classified into three main roles: the complete participant, the observer-participant, and the complete observer. The most attached form of engagement is the complete participant role, in which the researcher is completely involved in a situation. The most detached form of engagement is the complete observer role, which entails observation with no significant involvement in the situation or activity being studied. Between these two poles the researcher will be participating in the field but is semi-involved, allowing a level of research recording to be happening at the same time. In any research situation it is quite normal for the roles to shift in the course of research. For example, in some settings in worship (for example, in a large congregation) researchers may be able to maintain a high level of anonymity and be able to make notes and observe without active participation, then participate in corporate activity (such as singing, listening) whilst making observations, and then take part in ritual action in a way that they become a fully functioning member of the worshipping community (such as receiving communion).

By using the classification of roles you are in a better position to appreciate the stance you may be taking in relation to the research community. This is important for two reasons. First, your stance will influence the kind of information that is made available during the process of research. A complete observer will be able to record an account of the events of a ritual event but in comparison with the complete participant is in a limited position to understand the realities of ritual participation. You will need to decide whether such a limitation will have any bearing on your research question; for example if the aim of the research is to make a record of what happens in an act of worship the complete observer role is perfectly adequate (and could be supplemented by interviews to discover the reasons for the ordering of the worship event). However if you want to discover the inner dynamics of a ritual and explore how worshippers may experience it you need to become a complete participant. For example, if you were exploring the manner in which prayer for healing is administered and its impact on worshippers you may decide to participate in such rites.

Secondly, understanding the stance towards the research field will help you become more aware of how your presence may modify the activity being studied, a phenomenon known in the literature as 'reactivity'. There are two ways of approaching this issue. If you were to follow a 'naturalistic' stance you would try to reduce the levels of reactivity by making your presence in the research field as unobtrusive as possible. One of the arguments in favour of the complete observer role is that it holds the greatest chance of the researcher's presence being inconsequential, and so allows the situation to remain true to its natural state. However it is worth being aware that this does not always hold true. In small group contexts this argument is more difficult to sustain; a complete observer in a small prayer group would probably cause members levels of self-consciousness that would disrupt the normal life of the group. An alternative approach is to work with the reactivity and include it as part of your research data. Hammersley & Atkinson for example argue that it is impossible to do pure naturalistic research (because the researcher will always have an impact on the research field), and the wise researcher will pay attention to the ways in which the behaviour elicited by their presence informs them of the cultural life of the community. In certain circumstances this may be deliberately exploited for research purposes; a research project investigating the manner of welcome extended to strangers by worshipping communities could be conducted by researchers visiting churches and making observations of their reception as 'strangers' (though such covert research becomes increasingly difficult to do with the development of ethical rigour).

Researcher as Insider/Outsider
This discussion of a researcher's stance highlights the fact that, as in all forms of ethnography, the key research tool is the researcher. If you

become a participant observer you will need to understand the varied dimensions of your relationship to the community or situation you are studying. In the literature this has been classically expressed as the insider/outsider dilemma: to what degree are you an insider or an outsider, and what are the implications of each? In the case of researching worship, an outsider would have little or no previous working knowledge of the worship being observed. The challenge for the outsider is to attempt to understand the strangeness of the ritual through regular participation, and also through making use of other sources of information, such as conversations with participants and any documentary evidence that might shed light on the ritual (such as denominational commentary on the official understanding of the liturgy). Researching worship that is familiar to you, such as that of your own church or denomination, means that you work as an insider and benefit from a working knowledge of the norms of such worship. Whilst you may have an advantage over the outsider in terms of a better knowledge or acquaintance, it is possible that familiarity can dull the capacity to ask critical questions of elements of ritual practice that are taken for granted. Bordieu (1992, p.56) uses the term 'habitus' to refer to the routines of a community's life that have become second nature. Such patterns of behaviour are so deeply embedded that people are no longer conscious of the values and history that underpin them; actions have become simply 'the way we do things round here'. Making the familiar strange is an important task for the 'insider' researcher and this can be done in a number of ways. Visiting churches whose ritual differs from your own is one way of losing the naivety born of habit; through exploring differences you begin to be sensitized to the particularity of your own worship and therefore of its conditioned character. Another strategy would be to make use of a research partner who is a stranger to your worship. In his research on charismatic worship, Steven interviewed an 'outside observer' for whom such worship was totally unfamiliar, in order to sensitize the participant observation to the habits of such worship.

Observation

Being an observer is a role that we would regard as a natural human activity and at its simplest participant observation is the task of joining the activities of others in order to notice what goes on. However we should not assume the task to be straightforward. Social interactions are often sufficiently complex to make it impossible for an observer to capture everything that goes on, as will quickly become apparent to anyone wanting to give an account of public worship. One way to avoid being overwhelmed by the totality of the worship event is to refine the scope of observation. Even those research projects that begin with a 'soft' focus, asking the general question 'what is going on here?', normally develop a more refined focus as points of interest emerge through repeated observation. In observing worship your research interest may lead you to focus upon one aspect of the ritual, such as the role of leadership, music or the use of a liturgical text. Another way of managing the complexity of the worship event is to acknowledge that your account as an observer is a partial account, which, if it is to be regarded as reliable, needs to be cross-checked with the observations of others. This is why interview work is often regarded as a natural companion to participant observation, for it gives you the opportunity to check your observations against the accounts of other participants. This could be done by having a research collaborator (such as Steven's outside observer) or by interviewing the regular participants.

An important skill to be acquired for successful observation is the ability to become sensitive to the ritual dimensions of the worship being studied. One way of increasing your awareness is to read accounts of worship that draw upon ritual studies. Albrecht (1999) and Steven (2002) are two examples of studies that through participant observation have demonstrated ways of reading the ritual of contemporary pentecostal and charismatic worship. The categories used in both cases to describe the ritual dimensions would provide insights to studies of other more 'liturgical' forms of worship.

Another way to explore the ritual dimensions of worship is to use Susan White's questionnaire for religious ritual. In *Groundwork of Christian Worship* (1997) she lists 40 questions that could be asked of the activities in public worship, covering the use of space, objects, time, sounds, roles, and actions. These could be applied to your own research focus. For example, if you are interested in the role of musicians in church, your observation could be informed by the following questions: Where are the musicians situated (space)? When do they play and for how long (time)? Who are the musicians, how do they dress and how do they behave (identity)? Which instruments do they play (objects)? What kind of music do they play (sounds)?

Towards Analysis and Interpretation
The manner in which the research findings are analysed, interpreted and eventually written up as a coherent account of the worship being observed will determine the path by which the observations can reach their full

potential. Johnson (2005) in her article compares and contrasts two such approaches to handling information from observation, the anthropologist Jorgensen and the liturgist Kelleher. Both approaches aim to analyse and give an account of the field of study but differ in the way they view the end point of research. The anthropologist Jorgensen aims to turn analysis into a theoretical interpretation, which is then reported back to those being studied as a descriptive account of their reality. Kelleher wants to use analysis as a means of discovering what she calls the 'public horizon of worship' which is then judged for its theological and liturgical adequacy; for a working example of how this has been used in research see Steven (2002). The choice of which of these two approaches you take will depend ultimately upon your reasons for conducting research.

The main purpose of this chapter has been to introduce the main issues that need to be addressed by a researcher engaging in participant observation. Practical issues that have not been discussed, such as gaining access to a worshipping community, taking field notes and reporting back your findings to the worshipping community can be followed up in the relevant textbooks (see Bryman, 2004, and Hammersley & Atkinson, 2007, in the bibliography).

6. Interviews

Using interviews as a research method sounds simple – so simple that many people embark on it without the analysis and preparation that is necessary. So before you do, think about the why, what and how of interviewing as a research method.

Why are you thinking of using interviews? Are there data needed for your particular research that can best be gained by using interviews? Interviews can be costly in terms of both time and money, especially if the interviewees are widely dispersed or at some distance from your base. Recording interviews may mean carting two sets of equipment around (a back-up in case one fails when you are far from home), and certainly means hours spent afterwards listening, transcribing and analysing the material. Whether or not you transcribe everything will depend on time and the requirements of your study. It may be sufficient simply to note down some quotations that you can use. Bryman (2004) reckons one hour of interview needs five to six hours for this. And then there are all the problems of how you handle the interviews if people aren't giving you the information you need or really want to talk about something else!

So why do researchers use interviews? One advantage is that they get you directly in touch with people and help to 'earth' your research. Well handled, they can give you a great deal of data. They may also be creative in bringing out aspects of the subject you might not have been aware of, or thought less important. An interview can be more flexible than, say, a questionnaire, as the interviewer can follow up a train of thought. It can be a useful way of gaining detailed information from a small number of people, from an expert in the subject, or for example from the person leading an act of worship. Interviews can be used to take further or check out in depth the results of another research method such as a paper questionnaire. They can also be a rich source of quotes to illustrate or prove a point.

What is an interview? Is it more than chatting around the subject? Kvale (1983, p.174)[2] defines the qualitative research interview as 'an interview,

---

[2]   Kvale, Steinar (1983) 'The qualitative research interview: A phenomenological and a hermeneutical mode of understanding' in *Journal of Phenomenological Psychology*, 14, 171-196

whose purpose is to gather descriptions of the life-world of the interviewee with respect to interpretation of the meaning of the described phenomena'. That is helpful in making us focus on the double purpose of the interview: first, to gather information and second, to have an eye on the longer process of analysing, interpreting and seeing the emerging meaning when the jigsaw of all the interviews comes together to form a coherent picture. The quality of the descriptions gathered will have a large impact on whether or not the ascription of meaning is possible. Everything – the choice of interviewees, the preparation and conduct of the interview – will need to be geared to this end-product. That is not of course to say that you have to manipulate your data to fit your conclusion, or impose themes on them that make them appear coherent. In a post-modern world it is not always necessary to follow a pattern that goes from data through interpretation to conclusion. In some pieces of research the data may speak for themselves, or not be capable of being reduced to simple conclusions, and we need to be honest about that.

Interview modes

But what is the interview in practical terms? How is it done? You will need to consider the mode (looking at the advantages and disadvantages of each approach in relation to your subject), the content or design, and the manner of the interview.

There are currently three possible modes of doing interviews:

1. The face-to-face interview, sitting (preferably!) and talking to someone, or occasionally to two or more people, though if you tackle more than two it becomes more like a focus group or discussion and is more difficult to control. You can regulate the informality of the interview, the language and concepts used according to the person being interviewed, who can pick up signals from your face and manner. In the same way, you will be picking up useful information from their face- and body-language as well as from their words and accent. The way someone delivers a response to your question might display different degrees of enthusiasm or hesitancy. The immediacy of the interaction means that the interviewer has to concentrate on this multi-level response as well as formulating a follow-up question and keeping an eye on the time, as well as monitoring whether all the planned areas have been covered. Some might see the danger of exhaustion as a disadvantage, though the value of the immediacy usually outweighs this.

The main disadvantages, some of which we have already alluded to, are the need for recording equipment, the time taken in setting up as well as conducting the interview, the time and cost of travel. One possibility to consider is whether you might try to interview a number of people when they are together in one place, for example after a church service or a social event. But this will depend on whether the subject for your research requires a greater degree of privacy, either in their own home or by inviting people to come to see you. If you interview people at home, you may pick up more information that will contribute to your evaluation of their responses, but you will need to follow the usual protocols about the dangers of being alone with people.

2. Telephone interviews are – unfortunately for our purposes – something everyone is familiar with. They are useful because they take far less time and money, and enable you to talk easily to someone who is some distance away, or is less accessible such as a shift worker. They can be useful for example for following up or clarifying a point with someone already interviewed face-to-face. But the general distaste for phone interviews as a result of people doing cold calling will mean you will have to set up such interviews with great care, perhaps with a preliminary letter or electronic message agreeing a day and time for the interview. If you are going to make the information available to a third party (inevitable with most research) the law requires that you ask permission to record the conversation.[3] The main disadvantages are the reduction in the social cues available compared to the face-to-face interview, and the danger of interruption by callers or family. The problem of social cues can be partially overcome by using a video phone, or Skype voice and video calls, which also reduces the cost.

3. Internet interviews can be done in two ways. Using e-mail has all the advantages and disadvantages of sending out a questionnaire, though it is better than that in that you can respond and follow up easily with further questions. The disadvantages are that you lose the sense of immediate interaction, and may provide the interviewee with too long to think and to write essay-style answers! But capturing and recording the information is easy, as it is already in digital format. This is also true of the second approach, using the IM or SMS facility on a social networking site such as Facebook,

---

[3] This is the advice of Ofcom (see their website), based on the Regulation of Investigatory Powers Act 2000

Yahoo or MSN to have a real-time, rather than a delayed electronic interview. As with the phone interview, there is a reduction in social cues, but an agreement to use emoticons may supply a little of what is missing.[4] The use of such technology imports more flexibility into the interview process as it is accessible everywhere by mobile phone, though when determining sampling an allowance will have to be made for those not familiar with the technology. Apart from the straight interview, one possibility might be to set up a private chat-room where selected participants could share over a number of weeks their experiences or reactions, for instance, to the particular area of worship you are researching. For some discussion of the technical and ethical issues involved in using the internet it may be worth looking at websites such as Methodological Innovations Online, an international peer-reviewed research journal (http://www.methodologicalinnovations.org/index.html), edited by a team based in Plymouth University. They point for instance to the opportunities: 'The massive growth in social networks presents the research with many opportunities to study issues of social behaviour and attitudes toward privacy and security in a non-intrusive manner. Subjects happily post discourse and personal information for a public audience that provides invaluable insights into attitudes, social behaviour, group interactions and similar.' But they then highlight some of the ethical and security problems and examine ways of dealing with this.

Focus Groups

Focus groups are not strictly interviews, nor a fourth mode of doing them, but they do share some of the same aims (in accessing a wide range of data) and characteristics (in that they can be done face-to-face or using phone-conferencing or other electronic media), and need the same care in conducting them. They have an advantage over the one-to-one interview in being a more natural setting, and the fact that they are interactive sometimes stimulates the production of more data: as people listen to each other they learn to articulate things that may be only half-remembered or difficult to talk about. There is a good description of the effective use of this in research in a Pentecostal church in Cartledge (2010). They can also be cost-effective if you are researching in a small number of locations, and can be used to increase the sample size of a

---

[4]   Take care if your area of research is outside the UK or USA, as the emoticons may be interpreted differently in other cultures, or even in different cultural groups in UK.

report by talking with several people at once (Marshall and Rossman, 2006). But they can be difficult to control in order to get the data you need, and probably should not be used without some understanding of group dynamics.

Planning

Whatever mode of interviewing you adopt, you will need to plan. Proper preparation is the secret of the successful use of interviews in gathering research data. There are a number of preliminary decisions to take and tasks to be done.

First, whom are you going to interview? Both this and the next decision, about the content of the interview, are so closely bound up with your choice of subject for research that you will need, if you are doing academic research, to discuss them with your supervisor. If you are doing some other kind of research, for example for a local church or church group, you ought to discuss them with the reference group or commissioning group that set up, and will support you in, the research process. Particularly if you are doing only a small number of interviews, you will need to think about – and discuss with your supervisor - whether it is necessary to randomise your interviewees. If you need to look at a variety of sampling approaches, see Marshall & Rossman (2006), who list 16 types of sampling. Randomizing may not be necessary in qualitative research or for example if what you are doing is really a series of case studies, but for many studies it will be important to be open about your sampling method, and to be able to show that it represents the local population 'broken down by age and sex.' But the local demography may not be the important factor; with some subjects, for instance, it may be important to be able to demonstrate an even-handedness between different outlooks in a congregation, or between different kinds of churches over a larger geographical area.

Second, what questions are you going to ask? The interview should be designed so that it will produce the information you need. If all you are doing is collecting a random set of facts or ticking boxes it might be better to use a paper questionnaire instead. But you could design the interview so that there was a progression, for example from factual questions to deeper and more personal questions about attitudes and beliefs, as you develop a relationship and the interviewee begins to trust you and open up about things which may initially be difficult to discuss. Here you will need to be particularly careful to avoid manipulation: some people will develop a sense of what you want and give you answers in line with that.

There are some basic rules of question design, such as
- Only ask questions which relate to your subject. 'Do you like the vicar's hairstyle?' might not be relevant to your survey on attitudes to robes in church, and will give you a lot of extraneous data that won't fit in.
- Ask one question at a time. This makes both concentration and recording easier. 'Do you think the vicar should wear robes and that the choir should too?' will be confusing and make your work harder.
- Avoid built-in bias in your questions. 'Don't you agree that the vicar really ought to wear robes in church?' leaves no doubt which way you think they ought to answer the question, and will skew your results.
- Make sure there is some point to your question, preferably one that can be recorded. So 'What do you think about robes?' may be too general and confuse some interviewees who might not know whether you're talking about the Lord Mayor or what is worn in church. However, there may be a place for such questions early on in the interview, perhaps to establish the interviewee's general approach to the subject before narrowing it down to what you want to know.
- Decide what kind of answer you are looking for. You may be looking for fairly brief responses, particularly if you are intending to interview a good number of people, and need to have responses which are brief enough to be correlated, so that you can say how many people thought wearing pink albs was a good thing. But – and this is particularly true of in-depth interviews used as a follow-up to some paper-based research – you may want people to tell their story. 'Can you tell me a bit about how your attitude to people wearing robes in church has developed over the years?' invites a longer answer which may be rich in data.
- Work out the best order for your questions, and decide how long you think it is going to take.

Preparation

The third bit of planning is the more specific practical preparation. You will need to allow time for

- Setting up appointments, either by phone or letter, giving information which you may well repeat at the start of the interview about who you are, what your project – and the reason for it – is, how the results will be made public (if they will) and checking whether they are happy to be recorded and possibly quoted. It is good practice to use a consent form so that you have their signed approval, especially if you might quote them in a book or on other media. The form will need to be clear about whether you can attribute the quote by name. Not everyone will agree to be interviewed, but don't let that worry you, as you will have allowed for that in making your list of who to interview.
- Researching the background, perhaps of the place involved, or the interviewees, so that you can better evaluate their answers and be prepared with follow-up questions.
- Making practical plans about transport if you are doing face-to-face interviews, including getting and transporting recording equipment.

Conducting the interview

Beginnings and endings are important. If you take time to explain the process and to put people at their ease, they will be more relaxed and give you more help. If you don't, they may be defensive because they've not understood what is going on. Make sure the tape recorder is in as unobtrusive a position as possible. At the end you can signal that it is nearly over much more easily in a face-to-face interview by switching off the recorder or collecting your paper together. And be prepared, because sometimes it is just at that point when they will decide to unburden themselves about something really important that they've been holding back. You will then have to decide if they simply can't bear to let you go or whether this is something creative that will lead to a whole lot more relevant information.

Think through your own approach to the interview. You will give a clear message that the interview is not formal or confrontational (perhaps unlike some work interviews in their experience) by sitting alongside them rather than across a desk from them. The research interview is not the place for exercising power, whether that is professional-lay, man-woman, beautiful-ugly or whatever. You should have no presuppositions about what they are going to tell you. They are letting you into their world, for you to catch a little of their world-view, specifically in relation to your subject. So, whatever you feel about their world, you don't judge it but respect it, and you are grateful, and will show that gratitude. They may be mystified or apprehensive, but you want them to have a positive experience, and to feel that they and their contribution are valued. And if they go wandering off the topic and wasting your time, you will bring them back gently to focus on their experience in relation to your subject. All this demands a great deal of sensitivity, which you will need in order to develop the interaction and to look at information they can contribute which you might not have anticipated. Try to maintain eye contact as much as possible, rather than trying to write down everything they say (that's what the recorder is for). This again says that you value and are interested in them.

If you are interviewing over the phone or using instant messaging you will need the same attitude, but have to work harder as there will be less coming back to you by way of signals from the interviewee. You may need more often to ask process questions such as 'Is it OK with you to talk about this?' 'Am I going too fast?' 'Am I pushing you too much?'

Example: Interview about an Agape
Tovey (2009) -I- interviews a lay leader -L3b- about an Agape service held in the village church. The transcript has been cleaned up to remove ums, but does indicate pauses by...

I   Tell me something about this Agape thing that you do here.

L3b   Well we used to have a family service... and that sort of died really and we couldn't get the youngsters to come. And then the vicar thought it might be a good idea to have, you know if you have food with something it usually entices people to come.

I   Yes.

L3b   So we thought we'd try it and it must have been going for at least three years now I should think, or two and a half years.

I   So how often is this service?

L3b   Once a month. We don't have in the summer, July and August, but otherwise we have it basically once a month on the last Sunday and it's very informal. We have a table with a cross and a candle on, and we all sit round it on chairs... And we have the gospel reading and some prayers and we sing 2 or 3 songs, but sort of half way through we have coffee and croissants and orange juice. The children can come and ... play as they want to, or draw or, depending how old they are. And then we discuss the reading over the coffee and the croissants..., and then we finish it and we all, we have the intercessional type prayers, but we all each light a candle and say 'we light this candle for so and so or for something', or pray for, whatever. But you don't have to take part if you don't want to. I mean, if you want to light a candle you can, if you don't want to light a candle you needn't, you can just sit there and listen.

L3b   And that... it's that part of the Agape that sort of really gets to me, the prayer and the... lighting a candle to somebody or other.

L3b   I mean sometimes we have up to 20, other times we have about eight and, you know it just all depends. And the reader normally takes that... but we can, you know one of us can lead it if the reader's not there.

(Tovey 2009, pp.143-4)

Recording and analysing.

If you have several hours of material on a recorder you will need to listen to it several times in order to analyse what each interview says and how it relates to the thrust of your angle on the subject. Be prepared to modify your ideas as you go along. Sometimes it is a good idea to do some analysing before you have finished all the interviews, in case there is more data or a different angle that you need to pursue. At some point you may need to decide whether you are going to quote some people by name (with permission), or whether a series of unattributed quotes will have greater effect. And in the end, it would be courteous to let those you interviewed know the outcome, in general terms, of your research, and, if it is publicly available, e.g. on a website, tell them where they can find it.

7. Action Research

Action research is an interactive inquiry process that balances problem-solving actions implemented in a collaborative context with data-driven collaborative analysis or research to understand underlying causes enabling future predictions about personal and organizational change (Reason & Bradbury, 2001, p.1-14).

Let's expand and explain that definition in more detail. It is interactive and collaborative, so involves both researcher and participants in a journey. It involves collecting, researching and analysing data. This has two results: underlying causes are understood, and this leads to action. Something happens in the process of the research, so that it is not simply an objective appraisal of people and events. The something that happens may be problem solving actions being implemented, and it may lead to change in the people and organisation involved. So it is not something to be undertaken lightly or ignorantly!

The most common way for it to work is through the cycle: research and accumulation of data, analysis and reflection on the situation, construction of a plan for action, implementation of the action, review, collecting data on the results, and reflection leading to a further plan for action...in other words, a continuing process of change motivated by research into its effects. Do you have some secular examples or examples of who uses this?

One might ask why this tool for research has been little used in liturgical research. In the hands of a liturgically and sociologically well-educated and sensitive vicar committed to the principle of *ecclesia semper reformanda* you might catch a glimpse of an exciting church growing people spiritually and developing its liturgical life, with everyone involved in the process, which would take a number of years and would need sensitive external supervision. If you are a church leader and are tempted in that direction, then heed the warnings in this chapter, get a good supervisor, pray for the Holy Spirit and enjoy the roller-coaster...

Example of church-based Action Research
Martin (2001) provides an example of someone using action research to facilitate change in the life of a church. His experience

emphasizes the length of time (he took eight years) this kind of research takes, and that, to be effective, it has to be on-going. ' Some felt that the action research experience would be a once-and-for-all process that would solve our problems. After one cycle we would be "done". However, what we have discovered is that action research must be an ongoing cycle of planning-acting-observing-reflecting for us to remain relevant to a dynamic neighbourhood with high levels of transience. We are learning that we will never arrive at a "perfect practice" but must be in a continual cycle of reflection, planning, acting and observing'.

But for most people reading this looking for ways in to doing a discrete piece of assessable research, it is important to consider why this method is little used. We think that the key reason lies in its mixed nature, which in itself presents a danger both to the researcher and to the community in which it is practised. It is precisely because action research is a tool for changing communities rather than a 'pure research' tool of a more objective kind that most community groups and leaders (probably church committees, vicars, bishops or superintendents in the case of liturgical research) are reluctant to put it into the hands of MA or postgraduate students who have no responsibility for determining the direction, values and vision of the community. There is also the matter of time, as some pieces of action research will demand a greater commitment of time and involvement over a longer period than most MA or postgraduate students can afford. On the other hand, given students prepared to give that kind of commitments, who were also in a position to be trusted by the community leadership, they could play a vital role – which could then be written up – in acting as facilitators for the process.

One of the issues which is particularly highlighted by considering action research for research in a liturgical studies context is the 'scientific' nature of the method as used in social science. Batson (1993, p.379f) helpfully outlines the method and the problem. Scientific method usually requires a blend of three things: scepticism, empiricism and systematic research. Scepticism says 'OK, you have a good theory, but you need to test it by constructing situations in which it can be shown to be false.' Throw the negatives at your theory and report what happens. But that's not enough. You need to demonstrate that you've done this as openly and unequivocally as possible, in a way that is publically verifiable. That is empiricism. But even having publically verifiable empirical observation is not enough. The evidence for the theory must also be shown to recur on regular basis , and for that the research must be systematic. That is why scientists construct experiments which are causal caricatures. They are causal because they follow the 'if....then...'form: if you do x then y results. They are caricatures because they intentionally distort reality by manipulating some of the 'if' or x dimensions while keeping the rest stable, or neutralized, either by controlling the environment or by randomization.

Looking at social scientific method in this way demonstrates some of the difficulties in applying it to social science subjects, difficulties which are accentuated by the need to take both ethical and religious sensitivity seriously. We are unlikely today to follow the example of Lewin, Lippett & White (1939) in setting up a number of boys clubs specifically in order to research elements of aggressive behaviour! With predictable but unhelpful results... which is described by Leon Festinger (Festinger & Katz (1953), p.138). But Festinger's chapter on laboratory experiments might spark off some ideas, while reading it will make people more aware of the dangers and difficulties. Think about the problem of testing the correlation between a set of beliefs and a set of behaviours by randomly selecting certain individuals for exposure to those beliefs while preventing others from exposure. As Batson says, if you consider the beliefs to be of value, it would be unethical not to expose everyone to them; if the beliefs were dangerous, if would be unethical to expose anyone to them. This highlights the nature of action research, in being a kind of research which potentially changes its participants. 'Sociological research is behaviour: it is action which is covered and guided by rules' (Phillips, 1973). This 'method' is not something of passing interest, something to be corrected so that the 'bias' can be removed.

Bound up with the ethical-religious set of problems is how you resolve (and talk about in your resulting paper) the fundamental doubt about whether the people side of liturgy is a proper subject for research. If people are being changed by God in the course of worship, is it possible to get at that, and the evidence for it, without either undermining their belief in the change that is happening to them, or in some way contributing to that change? Susan White (2000, p.29) puts the dilemma in story form: 'When the great Dean of St Paul's Cathedral, William Ralph Inge, was [dining at a high table in Oxford and was] asked [by his neighbour, the distinguished liturgist E.C.Ratcliff] whether he was interested in liturgy. "No" said the Dean, "and neither do 1 collect postage stamps."' White says that, although it is usually interpreted as evidence of a wholly dismissive attitude to the study of Christian worship, it is much more a profound statement about the significance of worship in the life of the church. The most important thing about stamps is not their colour, shape, design, but what they do – so it is with worship. 'Worship is not simply another object for study, but a living breathing event of grace...' The way action research answers this dilemma is to acknowledge openly the involvement of the researcher in the process of changing people or situations.

The problems that lie in the way of 'true' experimentation lead some in the direction of correlational design, simply amassing descriptive data (and therefore using quantitative methods) in order to discover whether there are substantial parallels between bits of evidence. Amassing data may be preferred by some because it is less threatening to individuals and their beliefs and values, but doesn't necessarily provide and test theories which explain the evidence (Deconchy 1980). Others are led in the direction of designs which approximate to strictly scientific experimentation, for instance looking for non-random and naturally occurring comparison groups, or using time-series measurements of the same groups before and after significant events (Campbell & Stanley (1966)). If you are going to look for such groups (eg youth groups or home groups in different churches in the same area) and events (eg festivals, or a mission or a set of teaching sermons), then it is very important to be clear and up-front about the compromises and assumptions that are built into your research design.

As well as the ethical and religious problems involved in designing a piece of action research so that it in some way approximates to some recognizable 'scientific' or good research method, there is a major philosophical problem encapsulated in the term 'constructivism'. 'Constructivism assumes that truth and knowledge and the ways in which it is perceived by human beings and human communities is...constructed by individuals and communities.' (Swinton & Mowat, 2006, p.35). In other words, rather than the natural science assumption of a fixed, stable, external reality, it presumes that 'reality' is open to a number of different interpretations and can never be accessed in a pure uninterpreted form. It is an interactive process in which the researcher takes part, and in doing so inevitably changes and distorts the evidence. If this set of truth and knowledge is to result in action and change in either the community or individuals or both, then the way it is constructed has to be both interactive and cyclical. Provisional conclusions about evidence and proposed action need regular checking out with the participants. That is why it might be a lengthy process and why it needs very careful setting up.

So one result of looking at action research like this is to show that, because the research involves people and change, it can only be done with their full knowledge and consent. But how far does that consent have to go? It may be helpful to ask four sets of questions:

1. Whose agenda is driving the research? Is it the researcher's agenda? Are the participants in the driving seat? Is the researcher acting as the agent of an external body such as a denominational church leader who wants to see change in this community? If the participants have not asked for it, how is the project to be explained to them in such a way that they own it?

2. Is the aim and direction of the project clear? Where does it sit on the continuum from personal development to changing society? Is the aim limited to one age group or church or community (this is much easier to control and to write up) or does it have wider (and therefore longer) implications?

3. What precisely are the changes it is hoped to deliver? How are they to be measured or verified?

4. Is the cyclical and reflective nature of the research going to be handled in such a way that the participants will genuinely be participants? What control will they have over the research? For example, can they stop it at any stage, and if so, what effect will this have on the researcher and on her need to produce a report or to satisfy any financial backers that their money has been well spent?

Another – and more likely – result of looking at action research is that you will decide not to touch it with a bargepole. But you will be more aware of the danger of allowing your use of some of the other social science research methods to tip over into action research, and involving you in some of its dangers before you realize it.

8. Research Ethics

Questions about the ethics of any piece of research you are undertaking are very important. If your project is with a university, then you will have to conform to certain ethical guidelines and probably have to have an ethical approval. Independent researchers should conform to similarly high standards.

Principles of research ethics are easy to find on the net. One example is the policy of Oxford Brookes University (2000). This is based on two principles 'do no harm' and 'do good'. This is developed into a number of points the main ones being:
- No research should cause harm, and preferably it should benefit participants.
- Potential participants normally have the right to receive clearly communicated information from the researcher in advance.
- Participants should be free from coercion of any kind and should not be pressured to participate in a study.
- Participants in a research study have the right to give their informed consent before participating.
- Where third parties are affected by the research, informal consent should be obtained.
- The consent of vulnerable participants or their representatives' assent should be actively sought by researchers.
- Honesty should be central to the relationship between researcher, participant and institutional representatives.
- Participants' confidentiality and anonymity should be maintained.
- The collection and storage of research data by researchers must comply with the Data Protection Act 1998.
- Researchers have a duty to disseminate their research findings to all appropriate parties.

These points are discussed in fuller detail in the document.

Normally for interviews you should develop a consent form. It is often best also to have a sheet of information explaining what you are doing and the ground rules with which you want to work. You should obtain signed consent for an interview, particularly if you are recording it. There are particular issues in working with children and vulnerable adults. People need to know what you will do with the information, particularly if the results are to be published in some way.

Some have tried to justify covert study of congregations. Homan (1980) discusses an ethnographic study of a Pentecostal church, where the researcher did not say that any research was happening and pretended to join the group. The justification was that a direct approach to study the church would have been refused. This however is a weak argument and blatantly goes against the 'do good' principle. Churches can feel duped or betrayed if they discover covert study.

Some churches view their worship as a public occasion and so are open to observation. Other groups are more closed and will require permission to observe. Likewise some church documents are in the public domain, while others are private documents, which may require permission to read.

You might also like to think through issues of access for your research. Who needs to give you permission? Do you have a privileged access? In an interview do you have considerable power over the person being interviewed? For example, are you the minister interviewing your own congregation? How does that affect the interview?

There are many things to think through in the ethics of your research and you should do this carefully.

9. Conclusion

Our aim in this monograph has been to whet the appetite of anyone thinking of embarking on a piece of research and to convey something of our own enthusiasm for the use of sociological research approaches. There are simply too few pages to look at every possible method, and even those we have outlined may be subdivided into an increasing number of variations. But armed with our overview you can dig into larger volumes that describe and analyse different methods, such as Bryman (2004).[5] Not every sociological approach will suit itself to research into the people side of liturgy, but there is much to be gained from looking at examples from other areas of research, where there is a much longer history and therefore many more examples. As you read you will be making up your mind which methods suit your own sphere of investigation best. As you move to a decision, remember five things:

First, you will need to think about how at least two methods and tools might work. You will probably major on one method but using just one is not really safe. At the very least you need to use a second just to cross-check that the results you are getting are not simply a function of the research methods and tools chosen.

Second, be as rigorous as possible, while recognizing that people-centred research is always going to involve a compromise between rigour and finance and time, unless you have an unlimited amount of the latter two!

Third, consider whether you ought to trial a number of tools on a small scale, or trial some aspects of your approach, such as the wording of questionnaires if you are using them.

Fourth give sufficient time for the analysis of your results. You will gain impressions early on and you need to keep checking these against the data as it comes in as well as refining the conclusions. You need to make sure you have some clear conclusions that you can present to others in a reasoned way.

---

[5] Others include Aldridge, Alan and Levine, Ken (2001), *Surveying the Social World* (Open University Press, Buckingham): and Hughes, J.A. and Sharrock, W. (2007) *Theory and Methods in Sociology: An Introduction to Sociological Thinking and Practice* (Palgrave Macmillan, London)

Fifth, make a proper plan for your time before it runs away with you. Making time to plan is not wasting time, and without it you may face frustration when (as it does) the unexpected happens.

You are not on your own, and all five of these will benefit from discussion with your critical friend, supervisor, other members of your research community or sponsor group. You are part of a large community committed to raising the standards of research, and there is no reason why liturgical research should not match the very highest standards of research in other areas, not only in terms of rigour, accuracy and discipline but also in being adventurous, experimental and open to pioneering new theoretical approaches. This, under the hand of God, is our hope as we look forward to seeing a new generation of liturgical researchers, some of whom may be encouraged on their way by a monograph such as this.

Appendix: Bibliography

(Dates are here given against authors' names, as it is in this form that titles are cited throughout the Study, and they are accordingly listed by the chapters in which they are first cited, rather than alphabetically overall.)

Chapter 2

Albrecht, D.E. (1999), *Rites in the Spirit: A Ritual Approach to Pentecostal/Charismatic Spirituality* (Sheffield Academic Press, Sheffield)

Bryman, A. (2004), *Social Research Methods* (OUP, Oxford)

Cartledge, M.J. (2003), *Practical Theology: Charismatic and Empirical Perspectives* (Paternoster Press, Carlisle)

Cheetham, R. (2001), 'How on earth do we find out what is going on in collective worship? An account of a grounded theory approach' in *British Journal of Religious Education*, 23 (3), 165-76

Davies, Douglas James (2002), *Anthropology and theology* (Berg, Oxford and New York).

Flanagan, K. (1991), *Sociology and Liturgy* (MacMillan, Basingstoke)

Francis, L. J. & Robbins, M. (2003), 'Personality and glossolalia: a study among male evangelical clergy' in *Pastoral Psychology*, 51 (5), 391-96

Garrigan, S. (2004), *Beyond Ritual: Sacramental Theology after Habermas* (Ashgate, Aldershot)

Hoffman, L.A. (1987), *Beyond the Text* (Indiana University Press, Bloomington, USA)

Johnson, C.V. (2005), 'Researching Ritual Practice' in *Studia Liturgica*, 35 (2), 204-20

McGrail, Peter (2007), *First communion: ritual, church and popular religious identity* (Ashgate, Aldershot)

Mills, S. (2006), 'Extended communion: a second best for rural Anglicanism?' in *Rural Theology*, 4 (1), 23-35

Mitchell, N. (1999), *Liturgy and the Social Sciences* (American Essays in Liturgy; The Liturgical Press, Collegeville, USA)

Pitts, W.F. (1993), *Old Ship of Zion: The Afro-Baptist Ritual in the African Diaspora* (OUP, New York)

Quartier, T., Hermans, C.A.M., & Scheer, A.H.M. (2004), 'Remembrance and hope in Roman Catholic funeral rites: attitudes of participants towards past and future of the deceased' in *Journal of Empirical Theology*, 17 (2), 252-80

Ramshaw, G. (1996), *Liturgical Language: Keeping it Metaphoric, making it inclusive* (The Liturgical Press, Collegeville, USA)

Research and Statistics Department of the Archbishops' Council (2004), *Church Statistics 2002* (CHP, London)

Robbins, M. (2001), 'Clergywomen in the Church of England and the Gender Inclusive Debate' in *Review of Religious Research*, 42 (4), 405-14

Savage, A.M. (2001), *A Phenomenological Understanding of certain Liturgical Texts: The Anglican Collects for Advent and the Roman Catholic Collects for Lent* (University Press of America, Lanham, USA)

Steven, J.H. (2002), *Worship in the Spirit: Charismatic Worship in the Church of England* (Paternoster Press, Carlisle)

Stringer, M.D. (1999), *On the Perception of Worship* (The University of Birmingham Press, Birmingham)

Stuart, E. (2000), 'A Queer Death: The Funeral of Diana, Princess of Wales' in *Theology and Sexuality*, 13, 77-91

Swinton, J. & Mowat, H. (2006), *Practical Theology and Qualitative Research* (SCM, London)

The Catholic Church in England and Wales (2007), 'Catholic Statistics for England and Wales', <http://www.catholic-ew.org.uk/nav/stats.htm>, accessed 21/03

Tovey, Phillip (2003), *Inculturation of Christian Worship: Exploring the Eucharist* (Ashgate, Aldershot)

--- (2009), *The Theory and Practice of Extended Communion* (Ashgate, Aldershot)

Turner, R.E. & Edgley, C. (1976), 'Death as theater: A Dramaturgical Analysis of the American Funeral' in *Sociology and Social Research*, 60, 377-92

Wolff, R.F. (1999), 'A Phenomenological Study of In-Church and Televised Worship' in *Journal for the Scientific Study of Religion*, 38 (2), 219-35
Yust, K-M. (2007), 'Playing with Mirrors: Narrative Inquiry and Congregational Consultation', <www.religiouseducation.net/member/06_rea_papers/Yust_Karen-Marie.pdf >, accessed 19/03

Chapter 3
Ashton, P. (1984), *'For the Family' Report of the Bishop's Working Party on Non-Statutory Worship in the Diocese of Chelmsford* (Chelmsford diocese)
Astley, J. (2002), *Ordinary Theology* (Ashgate, Aldershot)
Astley, J. & Christie, A. (2007), *Taking Ordinary Theology Seriously* (Grove Pastoral Series. Grove Books, Cambridge)
Bell, J. (2005), *Doing your research project: a guide for first-time researchers in education and social science* (Open University Press, Maidenhead)
Bryman, A. (2004), *Social Research Methods* (OUP, Oxford)
Cameron, H. et al. (2005), *Studying Local Churches: A handbook* (SCM, London
Garrigan, S. (2004), *Beyond Ritual: Sacramental Theology after Habermas* (Ashgare, Aldershot)
Harries, R. (1995), *Pastoral guidance on the appointments procedure under the Patronage (Benefices) Measure 1986* (3rd edition; spring 1995 updated Nov 1997, CHP, London)
Hart, C. (1998), *Doing a Literature Review* (Sage, London)
Hopewell, J. F. (1987), *Congregation: Stories and Structures* (SCM, London)
Legal Advisory Commission of the General Synod (1997), *Legal Opinions Concerning the Church of England* (1st Supplement, CHP, London)
Schreiter, R. J. (1985), *Constructing Local Theologies* (SCM, London)
Tovey, P. (2009), *The theory and practice of extended communion* (Liturgy, worship and society series. Ashgate, Aldershot, Hants, and Burlington, VT)
Wolcott, H. F. (1990), *Writing up Qualitative Research* (Sage, London)
Young, S. (2008a), *The Use and Potential of the Daily Office in the Church of England: With Particular Reference to the Diocese of London* (Leeds)
Young, S. (2008b), 'Worship in Common? The Daily Office: from the Priest's Study to the Parish Church' in *Anaphora* 2 (1) 80-88

Chapter 4
Abbott, Pamela, Sapsford, Roger, & Sapsford, Roger (1998), *Research methods for nurses and the caring professions* (Social sciences for nurses and the caring professions; Buckingham; Philadelphia: Open University Press)
Ashton, P. (1984), *'For the Family' Report of the Bishop's Working Party on Non-Statutory Worship in the Diocese of Chelmsford* (Chelmsford diocese)
Bowsher, A. (2004), 'Christenings, baptisms and semantic confusion', <http://ia341321.us.archive.org/2/items/Christening_a_case_of_semantic_confusion/Xhristning.doc>
Bryant, A.W. (1983), 'Lay Communicants' Attitudes to the Eucharist in Relation to Liturgical Change in the Church of England', in D. Newton (ed.), *Liturgy and Change* (Institute for the Study of Worship and Religious Architecture, Birmingham) 75-97
Bryman, A. (2004), *Social Research Methods* (OUP, Oxford)
Francis, L.J., Jones, S.H., & Lankshear, D.W. (1996), 'Baptismal Policy and Church Growth in Church of England Rural, Urban and Suburban Parishes ' in *Modern Believing*, 37 (3), 11-24
Gillham, Bill (2000), *Developing a questionnaire* (Real world research; Continuum, London and New York)
Kay, B., Greenough, J., & Gay, J. (1993), *Communion Before Confirmation: A report on the survey conducted by Culham College Institute* (Culham College Institute, Abingdon)
Lee, R.M. (1993), *Doing Research on Sensitive Topics* (Sage, London)
Methodist Church (2009), *Children and Holy Communion*, <http://www.methodist.org.uk/index.cfm?fuseaction=opentogod.content&cmid=356>, accessed 09/06

Munn, Pamela, Drever, Eric, and Scottish Council for Research in Education (1990), *Using questionnaires in small-scale research: a teacher's guide* (SCRE publication, 104; Scottish Council for Research in Education, Edinburgh)

Oppenheim, A.N. (1966, 1992), *Questionnaire Design, Interviewing and Attitude Measurement* (New edn.Pinter, London and Washington)

Research and Statistics Department of the Archbishops' Council (2004), *Church Statistics 2002* (CHP, London)

Robbins, M. (2001), 'Clergywomen in the Church of England and the Gender Inclusive Debate' in *Review of Religious Research*, 42 (4), 405-14

Ross, K.R. (1995), 'Preaching in Mainstream Christian Churches in Malawi: A Survey and Analysis' in *Journal of Religion in Africa*, 51 (Fasc. 1), 2-24

Sims, O. S. (1999), 'Children's Worship: Empirical Research Findings on the Children's Sermon and Suggestions for Implementation' in *Review and Expositor*, 96, 549-64

The Catholic Church in England and Wales (2007), 'Catholic Statistics for England and Wales', <http://www.catholic-ew.org.uk/nav/stats.htm>, accessed 21/03

Tovey, Phillip (2009a), *The Theory and Practice of Extended Communion* (Liturgy, worship and society series, Ashgate, Aldershot)

--- (2009b), 'A Survey of the experience of leading worship of Reader candidates prior to training' in *The Reader*

Chapter 5
Albrecht, D.E (1999), *Rites in the Spirit: A Ritual Approach to Pentecostal/Charismatic Spirituality* (Sheffield Academic Press, Sheffield)

Bourdieu, Pierre (1992), *The Logic of Practice* (Polity Press, Cambridge)

Bryman, A. (2004), *Social Research Methods* (OUP, Oxford)

Hammersley, M. & Atkinson, P. (2007), *Ethnography: Principles in Practice* (Routledge, London).

Johnson, C.V. (2005), 'Researching Ritual Practice' in *Studia Liturgica* 35, 204-20

Jorgensen D.L. (1989), *Participant Observation: A Methodology for Human Sciences* (Sage Publications, Newbury Park)

Kelleher M.M. (1988), 'Liturgical Theology: A Task and a Method' in *Worship* 62, 2-25

Steven, J.H.S. (2002), *Worship in the Spirit: Charismatic Worship in the Church of England* (Paternoster, Carlisle)

Stringer, M.D. (1999), *On the Perception of Worship: The Ethnography of Worship in Four Christian Congregations in Manchester* (University of Birmingham Press, Birmingham)

Chapter 6
Gillham, B. (2000), *The Research Interview* (Continuum, London)

Beck-Lewis, M.S., Bryman, A & Liao, T. F. (2004), *Encyclopaedia of Social Research Methods* (Sage, London)

Cartledge, M. J.(2010), *Testimony in the Spirit* (Ashgate, Aldershot)

Jupp, V. ed., (2006), *Sage Dictionary of Social and Cultural Research Methods* (Sage, London)

Kvale, S & Brinkmann, S, (2009), *InterViews: Learning the Craft of Qualitative Research Interviewing* (Sage, London)

Marshall, C & Rossman,G.B. (2006), *Designing Qualitative Research* (Sage, London).

Tovey, Phillip (2009a), *The Theory and Practice of Extended Communion* (Liturgy, worship and society series, Ashgate, Aldershot)

Chapter 7
Batson, C.D., Schoenrade, P & Ventis, L. (1993), *Religion and the Individual* (OUP, Oxford and New York)

Campbell, D.C. & Stanley J.C. (1966), *Experimental and quasi-experimental* designs for research (Rand McNally College Pub. Co., Chicago)

Deconchy, Jean-Pierre (1980), *Orthodoxie religieuse et sciences humaines ; suivi de, (Religious) orthodoxy, rationality, and scientific knowledge* (Mouton, Paris)

Festinger, L.& Katz, D. (1953), *Research Methods in the Behavioral Sciences* (Staples Press, London)

Lewin, K.; Lippitt, R.; White, R.K. (1939), 'Patterns of aggressive behavior in experimentally created social climates' in *Journal of Social Psychology* 10: 271-301

Martin, Bruce (2001), 'Transforming a local church congregation through action research' *(Educational Action Research*, 9: 2) 261-278

Phillips, D.L. (1973), *Abandoning Method* (Jossey-Bass, London and San Francisco)

Reason, P., & Bradbury, H. (eds)(2001), *Handbook for Action Research: Participative Inquiry and Practice* (Sage, London)

Swinton, J. & Mowat, H. (2006). *Practical Theology and Qualitative Research* (SCM, London)

White, Susan J. (2000), *Groundwork of Christian Worship* (Epworth Press, Peterborough)

Chapter 8
Homan (1980), 'The Ethics of Covert Methods' in *The British Journal of Sociology* 31 (1). 46-59.

Oxford Brookes University (2000), *Ethical standards for research involving human participants Code of practice* (Retrieved from the World Wide Web:
http://www.brookes.ac.uk/res/ethics/ethics_codeofpractice.pdf/view)

The Alcuin Club
promoting liturgical scholarship and renewal
(see outside back cover)

The Companion to Common Worship (two volumes)
edited by Paul Bradshaw
*a detailed discussion of the origins and development of
each Common Worship rite together with a
comprehensive commentary on the text*
(Volume 1, SPCK 2001 - £19.99)
(Volume 2, SPCK 2006 - £19.99)

Celebrating the Eucharist
by Benjamin Gordon-Taylor & Simon Jones
a practical guide to the celebration of the Eucharist
(SPCK 2005 - £9.99)

The Use of Symbols in Worship
edited by Christopher Irvine
*a theological and practical guide to the use of water, oil,
light and incense in worship*
(SPCK 2007 - £9.99)

An Evangelical among the Anglican Liturgists
by Colin Buchanan
*a collection of the writings of one of the most influential
evangelical liturgists of our time*
(SPCK 2009 - £19.99)

To order any of these titles, or for details of how to join the Alcuin Club,
email alcuinclub@gmail.com or telephone 01763 248676.
For all full list of Alcuin titles, go to www.alcuinclub.org.uk
Generous discounts available to members.

Alcuin/GROW Joint Liturgical Studies

48-56 pages, £5.95 in 2008. Nos 1-58 by Grove Books Ltd, Ridley Hall Road, Cambridge CB3 9HU

Nos.4 and 16 are out of print. Nos 59 and following are published by SCM-Canterbury
– see outside back cover

Grove Liturgical Studies

These Studies of 32-40 pages ran in 1975-86, published or distributed by Grove Books Ltd.
The following titles are still in print. Price in 2010, £3.95

Grove Books Ltd, Ridley Hall Road, Cambridge CB3 9HU   Tel: 01223-464748

www.grovebooks.co.uk